dirty Boots MLJ SE

Dirty Boots / MLJ / SEArED
in association with
Pleasance
present

by Hywel John

World premiere at Pleasance Forth, Edinburgh, on 3 August 2011

rose

by Hywel John

ARTHUR
Art Malik

ROSE
Keira Malik

Photograph © Faye Thomas

Director	Abbey Wright
Designer	Richard Kent
Lighting Designer	Emma Chapman
Sound Designer & Composer	Alex Baranowski
Assistant Lighting Designer	Joshua Carr
Production Manager	Ali Day
Stage Manager	Connie Blackbourn
Dialect Coach	Tim Charrington
Movement Director	Ann Yee
Fight Director	Rachel Bown-Williams
Producer	Jessica Malik | Dirty Boots
Co-Producer	Alex Waldmann | SEArED
Publicity Photography	Faye Thomas
Cover and Publicity Design	Ben King
Cover Photography	Corin Hardy
Press and PR	Paul Sullivan PR
Production Assistant Coordinator	Francesca Moody
Production Assistants	Karl Brown, Ella Bolton, Tex Bishop, Aisha Josiah, Shanice Stennett, Anna Bilson, Omar Malik

Cast

Art Malik (*Arthur*)
Award-winning screen and theatre star Art Malik is one of this country's best-loved and most respected actors with a rich and varied career that spans thirty years in the industry.

Theatre credits include: *The Seagull* (Royal Court Theatre/Broadway); *Art, Indian Ink* (West End); *Othello* (RSC); *Trial Run* (Young Vic); *The Government Inspector, Romeo and Juliet* (Old Vic); *Timon of Athens, Destiny* (Bristol Old Vic); *Equus, A Man for all Seasons* (Liverpool Playhouse); *Cymbeline* (Manchester Royal Exchange).

Film highlights include: *True Lies, A Passage to India, The Living Daylights, Ghosted, City of Joy, Side Streets* and *Wolfman*.

Television highlights include: *A Jewel in the Crown, Upstairs Downstairs, Borgias, The Nativity, Poirot, Lewis, Second Sight, Messiah* and *Jackanory*.

Radio and voiceover credits too numerous to mention.

Keira Malik (*Rose*)
Keira recently graduated from LAMDA.

Rose marks her professional stage debut.

Theatre credits whilst training include: *O Go My Man, The Tempest, Love for Love, Romeo and Juliet, Women Beware Women, Memory of Water* and *Mixed up North.*

Television includes: *Secret Diary of a Call Girl, Secret Smile, Last Rights, Messiah II* and *Rockface*.

Photograph © Faye Thomas

Creatives

Hywel John (*Writer*)
Hywel John is a playwright and actor. *Rose* is his second play.

His debut play *Pieces* played to great acclaim at Clwyd Theatr Cymru in May 2010, before transferring to 59E59 Theaters, New York, in November 2010.

As an actor he trained at LAMDA and has worked nationally, in the West End and on Broadway.

Abbey Wright (*Director*)

Abbey was Resident Assistant Director at the Donmar Warehouse from 2008–09, during which time she worked with such notable directors as Michael Grandage, Alan Rickman, Jeremy Herrin, Peter Gill, Sean Holmes, Jamie Lloyd and John Tiffany. She was Staff Director to Danny Boyle on *Frankenstein* at the National Theatre in 2010–11.

Directing credits include: *Lakeboat* and *Prairie du Chien* (Arcola); *The Song of Deborah* (Lowry); *Hidden Glory* (Lowry and Tour); *The Ones That Flutter* (Theatre503); *Restoration Sketch Show* (Theatre Royal Haymarket). Later in 2011, Abbey will direct Conor McPherson's *Dublin Carol* for the Donmar@Trafalgar Season.

Richard Kent (*Designer*)

As designer credits include: *Stronger and Pariah* (Arcola), *Gin and Tonic* and *Passing Trains* (Tramway, Glasgow).

Richard has worked as associate to Christopher Oram since 2008, working on numerous shows at the Donmar Warehouse. As associate designer credits include: *King Lear* (Donmar Warehouse /BAM); *Red* (Donmar/Broadway); *A Streetcar Named Desire* (Donmar); *Hamlet, Madame De Sade, Twelfth Night, Ivanov* (Donmar West End); *Don Giovanni* (Metropolitan Opera); *Madame Butterfly* (Houston Grand Opera); *Billy Budd* (Glyndebourne); and the upcoming *Evita* on Broadway.

Later in 2011, Richard will design *Mixed Marriage* (Finborough) and Michael Grandage's farewell production of *Richard II* at the Donmar Warehouse.

Emma Chapman (*Lighting Designer*)

Emma trained at Bristol Old Vic Theatre School.

Recent theatre credits include: *Cosi Fan Tutte* (Royal College of Music); *All About My Mother* (RADA); *Dangerous Corner* (Bury St Edmunds); *The Machine Gunners* (Polka); *Bus Stop* (Stoke and Scarborough); *The Painter* (opening the new Arcola Theatre); a *David Mamet Double Bill* (Arcola); *Carmen* (Royal Northern College of Music); *Blowing* (Cambridge and tour); *The Maddening Rain* (Old Red Lion); Frantic Assembly at the Artsdepot; The Young Vic Schools' Theatre Festival.

Emma has worked on several plays at Trafalgar Studios amongst them the multiple award-winning *The Mountaintop*.
www.emmachapman.co.uk

Alex Baranowski (*Sound Design & Composer*)

Alex Baranowski is a composer, arranger and sound designer based in Central London. A 2005 graduate of Paul McCartney's LIPA, he recently worked with electro duo Underworld for Danny Boyle's *Frankenstein* at the National Theatre.

A regular contributor to the National, he was also composer for *Hamlet* directed by NT artistic director Nicholas Hytner and *Earthquakes in London* directed by Rupert Goold. Other theatre projects include: *The Merchant of Venice* (RSC); *The Faith Machine* (Royal Court); *Salt Root and Roe* (Donmar Warehouse); *Othello, Hobson's Choice* (Sheffield Crucible); and *Herding Cats* (Theatre Royal Bath). He has also recently composed the music for 2Faced Dance's *In The Dust* showing at the 2011 Edinburgh Fringe with a subsequent UK tour.

This year Alex's work in television and film has included five television commercials for Blue Dragon, *Made in England* for Channel 4 and feature film *NFA*. www.alexbaranowski.co.uk

Joshua Carr (*Assistant Lighting Designer*)

Trained at RADA in Lighting Design and Stage Electrics, Joshua now works as a freelance lighting designer and production electrician.

As lighting designer, credits include: *The Song of Deborah* (Lowry Studio 1); *The Shape of Things* (Soho Gallery); *Cinderella* (Young Actors Theatre); *Breathing Corpses* (Curving Road/Theatre Delicatessen); *Billy Elliot* (Young Actors Theatre); *A Clockwork Orange* (Fourth Monkey); *The Northerners* (Finborough).

As assistant lighting designer, credits include: *Lake Boat & Prarie du Chien* (Arcola); *Lidless* (Trafalgar Studios); *Ditch* (Old Vic Tunnels).

Ali Day (*Production Manager)*

Ali has been looking after people on stage and screen for twenty-five years. Her most recent credits include: The Comedians' Theatre Co production of *The School for Scandal* (Edinburgh, 2009); *Daily Cooks Challenge* for ITV and Punt & Dennis's most recent tour. She has long associations with both Arthur Smith and Antony Worrall Thompson.

Connie Blackbourn (*Stage Manager*)

Since her first professional job in 2005, Connie has worked in both Stage Management and Technical Theatre. Theatre credits include: *People – A Musical* and *Storm Large, Crazy Enough*. This will be her sixth time working at the Edinburgh Festival Fringe.

Jessica Malik | Dirty Boots (*Producer*)

Jessica returns to Edinburgh with *Rose*, her third Edinburgh production following the critically acclaimed Fringe First-winning *Guardians*, which transferred to London and Off Broadway, and *Angry Young Man*, which transferred to London's West End.

At Exclusive Films International she worked on such films as: Peter Weir's Academy Award-nominated *The Way Back*; Matt Reeves' critically acclaimed *Let Me In* and Daniel Radcliffe's much anticipated *The Woman in Black*.

She has recently launched her own film production company Pari Passu Films with Jessica Parker. She has worked as Associate Producer and Executive Producer respectively on upcoming films *Ghosted* and *January* (currently in production).

Alex Waldmann | SEArED (*Co-Producer*)

SEArED is the creation of actor Alex Waldmann (National Theatre, Donmar Warehouse, Almeida, Cheek by Jowl, BBC). It is an independent theatre production company dedicated to the development and facilitation of work that is provocative, politically conscious and, above all, entertaining.

In 2010, they co-produced Tom Wainwright's sell-out hit *Pedestrian* at Underbelly alongside Bristol Old Vic and Theatre Bristol. They are currently developing a new play *Colliery Row* with Liquid Theatre in association with Arts Centre Washington and Northern Stage (supported by Arts Council England), as well as co-producing the world premiere of *The Ducks* at Pleasance at Edinburgh Fringe 2011. www.searedproductions.co.uk

Thanks

The production team would like to thank: Corin Hardy, Ben King, St George's, Steven Packer and Caroline Rowe at Whittington Health, Nirjay Mahindru at Interact, HighTide Festival Theatre, Donmar Warehouse, Giles Smart, Myanna Buring, Richard Haigh, Elaine Walsh, Gina Rowe, Simon Shields, Ed Day, Choccy and Jessica Parker.

We would like to thank Jeremy Asher for his generous support.

Rose is presented in association with the Pleasance and was developed at the Pleasance's London studios in Islington. It was premiered at the new Pleasance Forth, at the Edinburgh Festival Fringe in 2011.

Pleasance Theatre Trust is a charity that supports and develops emerging talent and has provided a vital stepping-stone for thousands of young people wanting to work in the arts. It receives no public subsidy and invests all box-office income to provide a unique platform for the arts industry in the UK. Since 1985, the Pleasance has grown into the largest not-for-profit platform at the Edinburgh Festival Fringe. With twenty-six performing spaces in Edinburgh and London, ranging from fifty to eight hundred seats, the Pleasance has been able to present artists at the pinnacle of their careers alongside those just starting out.

For more information, visit www.pleasance.co.uk

ROSE

Hywel John

For Mum & Dad
with love

I have no interest in, much less capacity for, showing what the true Orient or Islam really are.

Edward Said, *Orientalism*, an Afterword (1995)

.

What's in a name? That which we call a rose
By any other name would smell as sweet.

William Shakespeare, *Romeo and Juliet* (Act II, Scene ii, 1–2)

'I have been given the authority over you, and I am not the best of you. If I do well, help me; and if I do wrong, set me right…
Obey me so long as I obey God and His Messenger. But if I disobey God and His Messenger, you owe me no obedience.'

Abu Bakr, from *On the State of Egypt*,
by Alaa Al Aswany, p. 45

We explain the signs in detail for those who reflect.

Quran; 10:24

For as others have oil and diamonds, we have the past.

Tristram Hunt, *Financial Times*, 28 April 2011

'I am from Iran, I was not happy there but I am happy here. For me, this is England. I love England, I love the Government, I love the Prime Minister, I love the Royal Family.'

Alan Rashidi, aged twenty-one,
Guardian, 30 April 2011

*He who wants to live in a cave will have the permission to live
in a cave. We have all kinds of monasticism.*

Pope Shenouda III

*In the sixties... when Muslims first arrived in the country, they
came here for financial reasons. They were economic migrants.
Their children, in the seventies and eighties and nineties, did
their best to integrate. They went to university. In the home they
were known as Akbar. At university they called themselves Bob.
They found white friends. And danced with them. And drank
with them. And slept with them. And took drugs with them. But
at the end of the day someone would call them a Paki.*

Omar Bakri Mohamad
(cited in Wazir, 2002: 32)

True Islam is democracy.

Alaa Al Aswany, *On the State of Egypt*

*'He is not an Orientalist, you know. He does not profess to have
more than second-hand knowledge there.'*

Will Ladislaw, in *Middlemarch: a Study of Provincial Life*,
by George Eliot

...history cannot be swept clean like a blackboard...

Edward Said, Preface to *Orientalism,* p. xiii

Characters

ARTHUR, *a father*
ROSE, *his daughter*

Note on Punctuation

A dash (–) at the end of a line of dialogue indicates an interruption by the following line.

An ellipsis (**...**) indicates an hiatus / a pause / a beat, the length and quality of which to be determined in rehearsal and performance. More often than not silent, but not necessarily still, and never empty.

Note on the Text

Italics are stage directions. If italicisation appears within dialogue, it indicates *emphasis*.

Note on the Design

There are two locations in *Rose*: a hospital room and a bedsit bedroom, both containing two beds. One set *must* be used for both locations.

This text went to press before the end of rehearsals and so may differ slightly from the play as performed.

Scene One

Night.

Late.

Very dark.

A hospital room.

A door and a window at opposite ends.

A small table, two chairs on either side.

Two single beds on either side of the room.

Curtain rails circle each bed. The curtains are pulled back against the wall.

There is a bedside unit next to each bed, with a couple of drawers and storage spaces.

ARTHUR, *lies in one bed, asleep. He is linked to a heart monitor, next to his bed – the wire from the chest pads dips out of the sheets and connects to the monitor – its line pulses silently.*

ARTHUR*'s bed is next to the window. The other bed, near the door, is empty.*

His bedside light is off.

A clipboard hangs on the end of his bed, an observation chart clipped on.

Clothes lie folded on a chair next to the bed – trousers, a shirt, socks. A bow tie sits on top. Next to the chair, a pair of old smart shoes, and an old-fashioned small leather suitcase.

ARTHUR *opens his eyes, blinking.*

In the darkness, a figure. It is too dark to make them out, but it is ROSE, *standing in the middle of the room, holding a small leather suitcase, identical to* ARTHUR*'s. She is smartly but simply dressed, wearing a simple hijab.*

ROSE. What have you done?

ARTHUR turns his head and sees her, but can't make out who it is.

...

ROSE goes and turns his bedside light on.

ARTHUR shifts violently in his bed, in alarm.

The heart monitor reflects this, its pulse quickening.

His movement is extremely restricted, but he can move his left side a little, in particular his left arm. He can move his head relatively freely, but he is bed-bound.

ARTHUR instinctively shouts out in fright, but the noise that emerges is extremely strangulated.

He struggles enormously to speak. He cannot form any words at all.

He seems to wrestle with his highly restricted movement and speech, whilst fixing his eyes on ROSE.

ARTHUR. Ooooo –

ROSE. What?

ARTHUR. Ooooo –

ROSE. What's that?

She sits on the chair.

He tries to shift away, but he physically cannot.

ARTHUR. Ooooo –

ROSE. No, shhh, come on –

ARTHUR. Ooooo!

ROSE tries to take his moveable left hand, or maybe touch his shoulders.

ROSE. Come on now, calm down, it's okay –

ARTHUR. Ooooo!

ROSE. Please, shhh –

ARTHUR. Ooooo –

ROSE. No, look –

ARTHUR. Ooooo –

ROSE. Please, listen to me –

ARTHUR. Ooooo –

ROSE. You need to calm down –

ARTHUR. Ooooo –

ROSE. What happened? –

ARTHUR. Ooooo –

ROSE. Listen to me, stop making that noise –

ARTHUR. Ooooo!

ROSE. No, fucking shut up –

ARTHUR. Ooooo!

ROSE. No, sorry, I didn't mean that, it's just I don't know what you're saying – you're not making any sense – has anyone told you what's happened?

ARTHUR *shakes his head.*

Oh, for fuck's sake –

ARTHUR. Ooooo!

ROSE. Sorry, I'm sorry, I know you hate me swearing –

He nods his head.

But you have to stop making that noise, stop trying to speak, it's not doing you any good –

ARTHUR. Ooooo –

ROSE. *Dad,* please!

...

Please.

...

What's happened, Dad?

He shakes his head.

You don't know?

He nods.

...

ROSE *sees the observation chart at the foot of the bed. She picks it up.*

This is helpful, lots of impenetrable numbers – Oxygen Saturation, Respiratory Rate, blah blah blah – gobbledygook, right?

You've probably guessed I haven't become a doctor.

She goes to his bedside table and opens the top drawer.

Or an accountant.

Or a judge.

Hello...

She picks up a clipboard with more papers attached.

She glances at it.

Oh, Jesus fucking Christ –

ARTHUR. Ooooo!

ROSE. Dad, now is not the time to get on my fucking back –

ARTHUR. Ooooo!

ROSE. What? How the fuck do you expect me to react when my father's had a fucking stroke?

She indicates the clipboard.

...

Sorry.

She drops the clipboard back in the drawer.

...

Sorry, Dad.

...

I can't f... I can't believe no one's told you.

...

Have you just woken up? Just now?

...

Dad?

...

Was that the first time you heard?

ARTHUR *nods*.

Fuck me...

ARTHUR *nods*.

...

Listen to me, you've had a... a really severe stroke, that's what that said, but you'll get better, okay? Okay?

ARTHUR. Ooooo...

ROSE. Please, it's no good –

ARTHUR. Ooooo –

ROSE. Come on, please, look at me, it's Rose –

He shakes his head.

Yes, it is, it's me, it's Rose –

ARTHUR *shakes his head in distress*.

ARTHUR. Ooooo...

ROSE. Nooooo?

ARTHUR *nods*.

ROSE *takes his hand and places it on her face*.

You see, it's me, flesh and blood. I'm here.

She holds his hand there.

...

It's me, you crazy old bastard.

ARTHUR. Ooooo...

ROSE. I'm sorry, but yes it is.

He shakes his head.

He points at her.

ARTHUR. Ooooo…

ROSE. What?

He points at her.

ARTHUR. Ooooo –

ROSE. Me? Ooooo?

He nods.

Rooooose?

He nods.

ARTHUR. Ooooo…

…

He touches her face, then gently pulls her head towards him.
ROSE *is led by him, and lays her head on the bed.*

He strokes her head.

He shuts his eyes.

Scene Two

Twenty years previously.

A bedsit.

Two single beds on opposites sides of the room.

8 a.m.

ROSE *resting her head on the bed, as before – her hijab on.*

ARTHUR *wakes with a start.*

ARTHUR. *Kem al waqt?* [What time is it?]

ROSE *wakes up with a start, leaps to her feet looking around her.*

ROSE. What, Daddy?

ARTHUR. Time, the time – what is the damnable time? Am I late?

What are you wearing?

ROSE. I –

ARTHUR. Take it off!

ARTHUR *advances on her, hand raised.*

Take it off before I – !

ROSE *takes off the hijab, retreating towards her bed.*

ROSE. No, Daddy, please –

ARTHUR. How did you – ?

ROSE. I… I –

ARTHUR. Do you want to drive a big rusty knife into my small puny heart?

ROSE. No –

ARTHUR. Do you want to scoop out all the pain and throw it onto my hard-working face?

ROSE. No, Daddy –

ARTHUR. Give it here.

ROSE. Daddy?

He advances on her.

ARTHUR. Give it here now!

ROSE *hands him the hijab.*

He goes to the bed, stands a moment, then he lays it out, and gently, slowly, precisely, folds it, then puts it under his pillow.

He stares at the pillow. He touches it.

Why did you not sleep on your bed?

ROSE. I don't know, I –

ARTHUR. What do you mean, you do not know? It is an easy question to answer.

ROSE. I –

ARTHUR. You have a bed, there it is – it is terribly wonderful comfy – I lay down on it myself in the bed shop and had the snooze to test it out. My dove, really, you cannot sleep in my bed any more, you are a big girl now. How old are you now, my Rose, my beautiful English garden Rose?

ROSE. Eight, Daddy, you know –

ARTHUR. No, I had forgot – whoops the daisy – I have a memory like the sieve. I try to forget many things. You know that, don't you?

ROSE. Yes, Daddy.

ARTHUR. My clever little Rose.

What are you?

ROSE. Your little Rose –

ARTHUR. The finest, most beautiful flower –

ARTHUR *and* ROSE. In the English garden.

ARTHUR. Clever girl.

...

How did you get the hijab from underneath my pillow?

...

ROSE. What – what's it called, Daddy?

...

ARTHUR. You will answer my question.

...

Don't be scared, remember I am the good King Arthur.

ROSE. You –

ARTHUR. *I*… I was fast asleep snoozing away into my dreams, my little one, I did nothing at all –

ROSE. Yes you did.

...

Yes you did.

ARTHUR. What did I do?

...

What did I do? It's fine, my little love, tell your silly forgetful father, I won't be angry – maybe I forgot, hmm? Maybe I had a bad dream and forgot?

ROSE. Yes, Daddy, I think that's what happened.

...

ARTHUR. Did I have another bad shouting dream?

ROSE. Yes.

...

ARTHUR. What did I say?

...

It is fine and dandy, my little darling love, tell good King Arthur, what did I say? I would like to know.

ROSE. No, cos you'll get angry –

ARTHUR. You will tell me!

ROSE. I woke up cos you were moving around a lot in bed and I tried to get back to sleep but I couldn't – and then you started to shout and I put my fingers in my ears so I couldn't hear you – but I could, Daddy, I could hear you, you were shouting out really loudly –

ARTHUR. Nightmare noises?

ROSE. Yeah, nightmare noises – funny weird words –

ARTHUR. Just some silly gibberish –

ROSE. Yes, Daddy, silly stuff, but then you shouted out this –

ARTHUR. What did I shout?

ROSE. This long noise, again and again – aaaaaaardaaaa – or something, Daddy – aaaaaaardaaaa – and I wished you would stop because I knew you were upset, but you wouldn't – and you shouted out more and more so I got out of bed to come and wake you up but then in the dark something hit me in the face and it was that... *hitch*... thing... I thought it was a pillowcase, Daddy – and then you went quiet all of a sudden – and then I took it with me to hold onto in bed cos I was scared – sorry I shouldn't have – sorry sorry sorry…

…

ARTHUR *sits on his bed, facing away from* ROSE.

…

ARTHUR *pulls a box out from under the bed, takes out a tatty shirt and starts to button it up. It is an identical shirt to the one folded up on the chair.*

And then I couldn't get back to sleep… Daddy?

ARTHUR *takes a bow tie out of the box and puts it on. It is an identical bow tie to the one on the chair.*

So when the sun came up I could see a bit more… and then I saw it wasn't a pillowcase – the… the hitch thing… so I just had a look at it – just a look – and I looked at my maths homework from last night.

Daddy? I looked at my maths homework…

ARTHUR *pulls some cheap suit trousers on, then his shoes and socks. Again, these items are identical to the ones on the chair.*

Then I was wide awake Daddy so I put my school uniform on and came and sat in your chair cos I thought you might still be scared…

Then I must have fell asleep…

…

ARTHUR. How did you know to put it on your head?

ROSE. Fareeda Banday puts this scarf on her head at school –

ARTHUR. A stupid question – let us forget it –

ROSE. And so does her mum – I thought it was the same thing – is it? It looks like it –

ARTHUR. Enough of this.

ROSE. Do you wear it on your head?

ARTHUR. No.

ROSE. Did Mummy?

...

ARTHUR. You are a clever girl.

We will not talk of this matter again, do you hear me?

...

Have you done your homework, my Rose?

ROSE. Yeah, I told you –

ARTHUR. Ah yes, you are clever and prepared, aren't you?

ROSE. Clever and prepared and ready to go into battle.

ARTHUR. Yes, into battle with the world. Why is that?

ROSE. For… for to live is to fight.

ARTHUR. And?

ROSE. And my brain is the most powerful weapon I got.

ARTHUR. I *have*.

ROSE. What?

ARTHUR. What did you just say?

ROSE. I don't know, Daddy.

ARTHUR. Yes you do, my dove, you just said it.

ROSE. My brain is the most powerful weapon I have.

ARTHUR. That's right, you prove your own point, my little wonder.

What will you do today at school?

ROSE. Don't know. Stuff.

ARTHUR. Answer me.

ROSE. Gym and maths and geography and English –

ARTHUR. Ah good! What is your favourite subject?

ROSE. English, Daddy.

ARTHUR. Good girl, my precious Rose.

'What's in a name? That which we call a *rose*'…

And?

…

And?

ROSE. 'And all the every' –

ARTHUR. No.

…

ROSE. 'And' –

ARTHUR. No.

…

ROSE. I can't remember –

ARTHUR. Yes you can –

ROSE. I can't – I'll be late for school, Daddy –

ARTHUR. This is school –

ROSE. But Daddy –

ARTHUR. This is school.

Now.

'What's in a name? That which we call a *rose*'…

My darling, this is yours, remember? This is your special poem, your new birthday poem –

ROSE *runs to her bed and pulls out a shoebox from under it.*

What are you doing? Put that back –

ROSE. But I'll just have a look at my birthday card and then –

ARTHUR. No!

That is cheating.

Are you a cheat?

Did I bring you up to be a cheat?

ROSE. No, Daddy.

ARTHUR. What is cheating?

ROSE. It is not cricket.

ARTHUR. Yes, my Rose, my English garden Rose. You are a clever girl –

ROSE. I'm late for school, Daddy –

ARTHUR. Do not be trying so very hard for my patience, young lady.

So.

'What's in a name? That which we call a *rose*'…

ROSE *looks at the box.*

That box will not aid you. The card can not help you.

ROSE. Yes it can –

ARTHUR. Insolence!

ARTHUR *grabs the box.*

ROSE *is tearful.*

…

Your mind…

ROSE. Is the most powerful… weapon… I have.

ARTHUR. 'What's in a name? That which we call a *rose*'…

ROSE. I can't remember, Daddy, I'm sorry.

He hugs her.

ARTHUR. Rose, my Rose, do not cry – say it with me, your birthday poem…

'What's in a name? That which we call a rose
By any other name – '

ROSE. ' – would smell as sweet.'

ARTHUR. Hurrah!

Hurrah! Say it with me!

ARTHUR *and* ROSE. Hurrah!

ARTHUR.

> 'What's in a name? That which we call a rose
> By any other name would smell as sweet.'

By the William Shakespeare, remember, my little love? No relation, it grieves me to report, but what is he? The prince of all the English writers. And which of his dramas is your poem from? Do you remember?

...

'Romeo and his Juliet.' It is very beautiful and clever. Like you. Isn't it?

ROSE. Yes, Daddy –

ARTHUR. You know why, my dove?

She shakes her head.

For it says even if you were not called Rose – my Rose, my little English garden Rose – you would still be as wonderful and precious as you are now. Is that not magical?

ROSE. I'm going to be late for school, Daddy.

ARTHUR. Not now, for now you may leave and there is still plenty of time I am sure –

ROSE. Sorry, Daddy –

ARTHUR. And I must go to work – no, do not be sorry, we got to the answer together, did we not, my dove?

ROSE. Yes, Daddy.

ARTHUR. And what are tears?

ROSE. Tears are the rain that waters the garden of life.

ARTHUR. My clever little girl. Now go to school.

ROSE exits.

ARTHUR goes to the bed and pulls out the suitcase from underneath it. He opens it and takes out a half-empty bottle of whiskey. He opens it, pouring a small amount into a cup on his bedside table. He puts the whiskey back in the case and puts it back under the bed.

He sits on the bed.

He drinks his whiskey in one gulp.

...

He takes the hijab out from under the pillow.

He smells it.

He pulls the sheets over him, clutching the hijab.

Scene Three

Back to now, the hospital.

Night.

Later.

ARTHUR *opens his eyes.*

ROSE *stands in the middle of the room, holding her suitcase.*

She wears a hijab.

ARTHUR *shifts in his bed in alarm.*

ARTHUR. Ooooo –

ROSE. Yeah, here I am.

Remember this old thing?

Matching suitcases. Like we're going to the seaside again.

Is that where you were going?

Dad? Come on, answer me.

He looks away.

Oh fuck, sorry.

He looks back and glares.

Yeah yeah, sorry, sorry.

He looks away.

ROSE *goes to his suitcase and pulls it out from under his bed.*

ARTHUR. Ooooo!

She opens it up.

ROSE. Give it a rest, I'm having a look and there's not a huge amount you can do about it –

She lifts out the whiskey.

What a surprise…

She puts it on his bedside table.

If you want a drink, you're going to have to ask politely.

She goes back to the suitcase, rifling through it.

Pants, pants, pants… some more pants… two identical shirts… three bow ties… a copy of *Romeo and Juliet*, of course…

A small snapshot falls out of the book.

Hello… Look at that, a photo of me. Fuck me, I haven't changed a bit. How old am I there? Eight?

ARTHUR *nods.*

Thought so.

She rests the photo against the whiskey bottle, then goes back to the suitcase.

A toothbrush… a razor… socks…

Is this all you've got left?

Dad?

He looks away.

If you could speak, would you tell me where you were going?

He does not look around.

Course you wouldn't.

Dad, look at me for a second, would you?

He turns to look at her.

Look… I could sleep in that other bed if you want.

If you'd like me to stay here and keep you company.

If you'd like that.

I've brought my stuff, haven't I? It'll be like old times.

She picks up her suitcase.

So? Would you like that?

He looks away.

Dad?

Right.

Unbelievable. Fucking unbelievable.

ARTHUR *looks at her sharply.*

What? It is, it's fucking unbelievable – I offer to stay here, to mop your fucking brow and what do I get? The same old shit. You know what? I'm going to sleep right there, because I *know* that's what you want. And I'm going to stay until you can open that ranting old mouth of yours and tell me to fuck off. Alright?

He nods.

Thank you.

She goes and sits on the other bed, holding her suitcase.

He looks away.

Scene Four

Eighteen years before.

Sunrise.

ROSE *is sitting on her bed, her suitcase next to her. She wears no hijab.*

ARTHUR *is asleep, tucked up in bed.*

The half-empty whiskey bottle is on the bedside table.

Very quietly, ROSE *opens her suitcase and takes out a square of fabric.*

ARTHUR *turns in his sleep.*

She shoves the fabric back in her suitcase and stays very still.

ARTHUR *remains asleep.*

ROSE *takes out the fabric again and lays it on her lap. The fabric is frayed around half of its edges. The other half has been slightly folded in and sewed on, to create a smooth edge.*

She constantly keeps an eye on the sleeping ARTHUR.

She picks up the fabric and drapes it over her head, pinching it together under her chin to check the length – revealing the basic shape of a hijab.

She lays it on her lap again, takes a needle and thread from her suitcase, and continues to sew up the edge.

After a moment, whilst checking on ARTHUR, *she accidentally pricks her thumb with the needle.*

ROSE. Ah!

    ARTHUR *turns in his sleep.*

    ROSE *shoves the fabric back in her suitcase and shuts the lid, making a noise.*

    ARTHUR *wakes with a start.*

ARTHUR. Time, what time is it?

    ROSE *sucks her bleeding thumb.*

    ...

ROSE. Sunrise, Daddy.

ARTHUR. My darling dove, why are you awake with the sun?

ROSE. Don't know.

ARTHUR. Don't suck your thumb, you are not a baby.

    ROSE *sits on her hand.*

    Did you have a nightmare?

ROSE. No.

ARTHUR. Were you doing homework?

ROSE. No.

ARTHUR. Could you not sleep soundly?

ROSE. No.

ARTHUR. Ah.

I slept like the log.

ROSE. You snored again.

ARTHUR. Snoring is the noise of happy dreams, so it must be cultivated, not cursed.

ROSE. I didn't curse it, Daddy.

ARTHUR. No, my Rose, but if what you just said was music, it had a melancholy tune.

ROSE. I think you snored because of all the whiskey you drank last night.

...

ARTHUR. You are a clever girl.

...

Whiskey can be medicine. The Scots, a noble race, drink it for health and vitality. This I am told, my little wonder. Marcus, he who works the forklift truck at the warehouse, Marcus is a Scot, and when he is of ill-health, he drinks of the whiskey. He says it fires the engine of his constitution. And what is a constitution, my clever little Rose?

ROSE. I don't know, Daddy.

ARTHUR. This is advance-level knowledge, my little one. Constitution is what Government is made of. And Government, Democracy, is what makes England, our home, so marvellous. For Constitution is the heart of Democracy, and Democracy is the heart of England, and England is where our heart belongs, correct?

ROSE. Yes, Daddy.

ARTHUR. So if Marcus the Scot says whiskey fires his constitution, he is saying it is good for his heart, for his Government, and so for England. And that is wisdom I am happy to absorb, even if he only drives the forklift truck and is otherwise a fool.

...

For a wise person listens even to the words of fools, my clever little dove.

ROSE. Yes, Daddy.

ARTHUR. Well, here we are, up with the cock-a-doodle-doos and the whole day in front of us. I am not hungry yet, what about you, my sweet, do you want some crumpets or a muffin?

ROSE. No thank you, Daddy.

ARTHUR. I have a headache from the infernal whiskey.

ROSE. I thought it was good for the Government?

...

You slept in your clothes again, Daddy.

ARTHUR. I had a chill. Still I am not used to the charming English climate after all these years. But you, you are made of sterner stock. Now tell me, why have you got your travelling suitcase on your bed, my dove?

...

Answer me.

ROSE. Because we're going to the seaside today for my birthday treat.

Aren't we, Daddy?

You said so last weekend.

You said last night.

...

ARTHUR. Yes, of course, it is your birthday. Of course it is. Your birthday. You are nine – no, you are ten today – yes – no – how old are you?

ROSE. Ten.

ARTHUR. I am jesting with you. Of course, you are ten – the double figures at last – one step closer to adulthood and the glorious future. Hurrah!

Say it with me. Hurrah!

ARTHUR *and* ROSE. Hurrah!

ARTHUR. Oh, my clever little girl, well done for you, well done for remembering so accurately when your birthday is – you know how my head often is living – where is it living most of the times?

ROSE. In a fog.

ARTHUR. Yes! In the fog and the mist, because I am turning into the old fart, as they say, and I am working all the hours of the day and there are so many important things I must remember as I continue to become a good English citizen just like you, but sometimes the smaller things, such as numbers, mathematics, birthdays… they fall through the sieve in my brain. Straight through! Down the drain! I have no thoughts for them. For what is my true work, if I am not to be in the warehouse to put the food on our table?

ROSE. A bookseller.

ARTHUR. Yes, my clever girl, you know your father like the back of my hands. I was bookseller – I mean, I will become a bookseller, I want to become a bookseller – I will be, one day soon…

…

But you, my little wonder, are a mathematic wizard, like the Merlin and Professor Stephen Hawking, and you remember all those little numbers, those silly little… trifles! Mere trifles! And when you are a grown lady you may choose if you wish to be an accountant, or a mathematics teacher, or an economist, or a policewoman –

ROSE. Can we go swimming in the sea, Daddy?

ARTHUR. Of course you can.

ROSE. Will you come with me?

ARTHUR. I… I will… what the word is? Paddle in, yes, I will paddle in. Like the King of Canute.

ROSE. Who's that?

ARTHUR. An English king who ruled the oceans and the seas.

ROSE. I thought you were the good King Arthur?

ARTHUR. I am both.

ROSE. Danny Simpson says I can't go in the sea cos Pakis can't swim – can you swim?

ARTHUR. Who says that?

ROSE. Danny Simpson.

ARTHUR. I thought Danny Simpson was your ally in the playground?

ROSE. He is.

ARTHUR. Then why this little idiot call you a Paki?

ROSE. I punched him in the nose.

ARTHUR. You did what?

ROSE. I punched him in the nose and made it bleed.

ARTHUR. Never do that.

ROSE. Why not? He called me a Paki.

ARTHUR. So what? He is a fool.

ROSE. Don't say that, he's my friend.

ARTHUR. But he insulted you.

ROSE. Yeah, but he said sorry, anyway he's my friend really. And he's fat, so he can't talk.

ARTHUR. Why not? Is he so fleshy around his mouth that no sound is emitted?

ROSE. That's not what I mean.

ARTHUR. How fat? Roly-poly like the Michelin Man in the adverts?

ROSE. Yeah.

ARTHUR. Fat like a sweaty doughnut?

ROSE. Stop it!

ARTHUR. Promise me never to hit Danny Simpson again.

ROSE. Why?

ARTHUR. Why do you think violence will help you? Violence will not help you.

ROSE. It made him say sorry.

...

ARTHUR. Did he know the violence was approaching?

ROSE. What, Daddy?

ARTHUR. Did you warn him?

ROSE. Don't be stupid.

ARTHUR. What is that you say to me?

...

ROSE. Sorry.

ARTHUR. Heavens above.

Was it courageous?

Was it noble to punch Danny the Doughnut's nose without his invitation?

ROSE. I don't understand – it's my birthday...

ARTHUR. There will be no paddling with King Canute today if you do not heed this lesson. What is better – to flatten Fat Danny in unthought anger and indignation? Or to say to him, 'Danny, you are wrong, I am not a Paki, but your intentions in calling me so are nothing but the most common insult, for you demean and lessen me by such a label. So I hereby challenge you to a duel.'

What is the correct answer?

ROSE. To challenge him to a duel?

ARTHUR. Correct, yes, a duel. Or a joust.

> For then you may still inflict righteous vengeance upon him, but you have risen divinely above his puerile, small-minded bigotry by giving him fair and reasonable warning of his impending punishment. You become an Englishman with such behaviour. Danny Simpson is no Englishman.

ROSE. So we're not Pakis then?

> ...

> What are we then?

ARTHUR. English, of course.

ROSE. We don't look very English. Danny Simpson looks English – so does Sophie Epstein.

ARTHUR. What have looks to do with anything? What is your name?

ROSE. Rose.

ARTHUR. Rose what?

ROSE. Smith.

ARTHUR. Thank you. And what is mine?

ROSE. Arthur Smith.

ARTHUR. Answer me this, my wondrous little girl – could there be two more English names in the whole of this fair and free country?

ROSE. Um –

ARTHUR. The answer is a firm and unwavering no.

ROSE. So we're not Pakis?

ARTHUR. Today I set you a birthday challenge –

ROSE. I don't want to do a birthday challenge –

ARTHUR. Today we will walk out into the world together and board the train for the seaside and from hereon in I shall only call you Rose and you shall only call me Arthur and we shall see how many people do not think we are English. Psh. Not English... Look at your passport, you will see where you are from.

ROSE. Have you got a passport, Daddy?

ARTHUR. Ah! What is my name?

ROSE. We haven't left yet.

ARTHUR. The challenge begins now!

...

ROSE. Have you got a passport… Arthur?

ARTHUR. I… No.

ROSE. Why not, Arthur?

ARTHUR. Why would I want to leave this green and pleasant land, Rose?

ROSE. Can we become Pakis if we want?

ARTHUR. You can become whoever you want, but you are a clever girl, so do not use this stupid word.

ROSE. Fareeda Banday said she's a Paki and so am I.

ARTHUR. You are not.

ROSE. But she wears a… a hijab and so does her mum – just like Mummy's one under your pillow –

ARTHUR. You think this proves something? Huh? This is some *Paki proof* for you? You do not know whereof you speak. You are a beautiful girl, but your ignorance is ugly.

...

ROSE. So is Fareeda a Paki?

ARTHUR. No, she is not. No one is.

ROSE. But she's from Pakistan.

ARTHUR. So she is Pakistani, not a Paki.

ROSE. What's the difference?

ARTHUR. The difference is Danny Simpson's bloody nose.

...

ROSE. Danny Simpson says if you unscrew your belly button your bum falls off.

ARTHUR. In this he is correct, indubitably.

ROSE. Thought so.

...

Can Pakis swim then?

ARTHUR. Of course they can, although there is every democratic chance some of them may not be able to swim very well.

ROSE. Is that why you only want to paddle, Daddy?

...

After he said sorry, Danny Simpson said it's okay if Pakis can't swim, because white men can't jump.

ARTHUR. I am unsurprised Danny the Doughnut cannot jump.

...

ROSE. Is it too early to go, Daddy?

ARTHUR. It is never too early for my little Rose's birthday treat –

ROSE. Can we do presents now before we go?

ARTHUR. What?

ROSE. Can we do presents now before we go, Daddy?

ARTHUR. Ah...

Yes...

He looks around the room.

How would you like to... to take a taxi today? Like a wealthy English lady. How would you like that?

...

ROSE *sits down on her bed, clutching her bag.*

We will beckon a taxi, a handsome cab, a hackney carriage, and we shall travel to the train like... like a king and queen. How is that? How is that for a present?

...

ROSE. Would you like to sleep some more before we go to the seaside, Daddy?

ARTHUR. What, my dove?

ROSE. It's still early and I know you work very hard.

...

ARTHUR. Look at you, my clever little girl. You know what's good for your father.

ROSE. I'll wake you up when it's time to go. Then we can get a taxi if you want.

ARTHUR. Yes, yes, a taxi carriage –

ROSE. Yes, Daddy –

ARTHUR. To the seaside –

ROSE. Yes, Arthur.

...

ARTHUR. Yes, my Rose, my darling little Rose.

...

He climbs into bed and turns towards the wall.

Scene Five

Now.

The hospital.

Night.

Very late.

ARTHUR *wakes with a start, turning to see if* ROSE *is still there.*

She sits on the bed still clutching her bag, but the hijab is now on.

ROSE. I'm not tired.

You should go back to sleep, Dad, you must be knackered.

ARTHUR *shakes his head.*

No?

You never managed to sleep very soundly, did you?

He shakes his head.

I can't remember a single clear night. You screamed a lot, do you know that?

He nods.

Yeah, course, I used to report back every morning, didn't I? When I was little. When I was a girl.

It never stopped, you know. I know I stopped telling you, but it never…

He looks away.

You knew that though, didn't you?

Yeah, you knew.

I did start to sleep through it after a while. Sort of. I mean, fuck, I'd hear it, but after a while it just became… *noise.* Yeah. Like a TV buzzing away in the background. White noise, isn't that what it's called?

Not in our home.

What then?

English noise.

Englishnoise.

Englishness.

That's you, isn't it?

He nods.

You like that?

He nods.

Course you do, King Arthur.

Sorry, Dad. Go back to sleep.

He shakes his head.

What am I thinking? Trying to tell you what to do. What a fucking idiot.

ARTHUR. Ooooo!

ROSE. Oh, give it a break would you, Arthur? I swear, alright? People do. *English* people do.

What? I know it's crude and simple and – what would you say? – *ignoble*, but I don't care, Dad, that's why I like it.

That's why I cunting well like it.

ARTHUR. Ooooo!

ROSE. Sorry. That was a cunt too far.

He turns away.

You're right – I should go to sleep.

She gets undressed, taking off the hijab, and chucks her clothes on the bottom of the bed in a pile.

He turns and sees her in her underwear. He watches her.

She opens her bag, picks out a nightie and puts it on.

As she undresses and dresses –

I don't get it though, Arthur, you love the English language so much – this *foreign* language – your *second* language – you flap about in it like you're drowning, but always with a smile on your face. Yet you can't bear swearing. Doesn't make sense to me. I mean, I'm a clever girl, right? So I can appreciate it.

She gets into bed.

Night, Dad.

She turns off her bedside light.

...

Fuckhead.

I love that one.

Get it?

It's pretty simple, imagine someone has a fuck as a head.

Actually, I dunno how that's possible.

How about… *cuntlips*.

Great.

Fairly straightforward, right? Slang expression for the vaginal labia.

Don't be squeamish, Arthur, I know you've already figured these out. You remember.

And on a similar theme… remember this one? Very appropriate… *camel toe*.

No?

It means…

Doesn't matter.

…

How about…

(*Softly*.) Waaaaaardaaa…

Waaaardaaa….

Scene Six

Sixteen years previously.

The bedsit.

Night.

Late.

Dark.

Both in bed asleep.

ROSE *shifts in bed, seems to wake. Movement under the sheets.*

Suddenly, a terrified discovery –

ROSE. Aaaaaaaaaaaaah!

ARTHUR *wakes with a sudden jolt.*

ARTHUR. Warda?

ROSE. Aaaaah!

ARTHUR. Rose?

He turns on his light.

ROSE *is crying.*

Rose, my dove, what is wrong –

ARTHUR *leaps out of bed and runs to her.*

ROSE. No, Daddy, I'm alright –

ARTHUR. You are crying –

ROSE. No –

ARTHUR. You scream out –

ROSE. Daddy, no no no, I'm fine –

ARTHUR. That was not the noise of fine –

He tries to pull the sheets back, but she resists.

ROSE. No, Daddy –

ARTHUR. You are crying, my little dove – come here –

ARTHUR *pulls back the sheets and goes to pick her up, but steps back hurriedly in shock.*

ROSE *has menstrual blood on her nightie.*

Oh…

ROSE *pulls back the sheets to cover herself.*

I…

ARTHUR *goes to his own bed and sits down, facing away from* ROSE.

…

ARTHUR *starts to shake.*

ROSE. Daddy?

ARTHUR *controls himself.*

ARTHUR. My darling dove, are you alright?

ROSE. Don't worry, I know what it is –

ARTHUR. You want me to phone the ambulance men?

ROSE. No, Daddy, don't be silly –

ARTHUR. Do not be proud, NHS is free medical help, welfare
state to help all English citizens, you are no different –

ROSE. No, Daddy –

ARTHUR. Are you in pain, lots of pain?

ROSE. Only a little bit.

He goes to the phone next to his bed.

ARTHUR. I phone the ambulance –

ROSE. Dad, don't, you don't need to –

ARTHUR. Hello? 999?

ROSE. Dad –

ARTHUR. I have a medical emergency, please, yes –

ROSE. Dad, Dad, put the phone down –

ARTHUR. It is my daughter, I am very worried –

ROSE. Dad!

ARTHUR. Yes, that is her, you must listen to me, please –

ROSE. Dad, it's just my period!

ROSE *gets out of bed and goes to* ARTHUR.

ARTHUR. You see very similar thing happen to her mother –

ROSE. Dad!

ROSE *takes the phone out of his hand and puts it down on
the handset.*

What are you doing?

He picks up the phone again.

She grabs it.

No!

They tussle with the phone.

ARTHUR. You are grievously ill – listen to your father –

He pushes her away.

ROSE. It's just my first period, Dad!

ARTHUR *notices she's standing in her bloodstained nightie.*

ARTHUR. Aaaaaah –

He drops the phone and stumbles back in fright.

ROSE *steps back at his shock.*

ARTHUR *falls over the bed onto the floor, then leaps up.*

Illa jaheem! [Damn it to hell!]

They stand at opposite ends of the room.

I have seen this before – you are being an ignoramus –

ROSE. Lots of my friends have had them already, I was just frightened because it hurt loads when I woke up –

ARTHUR. You do not feel what I feel – you think you are such of a clever clogs –

ROSE. I'm twelve years old – I learnt about it in biology class – I was just scared –

ARTHUR. I am not stupid, I am not ignorant – I feel what it is to be a woman.

...

ROSE. No you don't.

ARTHUR. What, because I am not a woman?

ROSE. Yeah.

ARTHUR. Congratulations to you, Sherlock Holmes, your logic is empirical, unbreakable – you are right – I am a man, I am your father, but you are not a woman yet. Soon, but not yet. You are a child. So do not tell me what I feel.

ROSE. I wish I had a mum.

ARTHUR. So do I.

ROSE. You can't know! You can't know about this! You big…
fucking idiot!

He slaps her across the face.

…

ARTHUR. You will never speak such things to me.

ROSE *begins to cry.*

He holds her by the shoulders and looks directly at her.

Yes, you cry. You should.

You are growing up, my Rose. It hurts, yes?

Yes?

She nods.

Your anger is just and right. You think, what is this old
buffoon talking about? How can he know what it is to become
a woman. Well, I cannot. You are right. I cannot *know*. But this
I did not claim, my little soldier. What did I claim?

What did I claim?

Answer me.

ROSE. I dunno.

ARTHUR. You what? You *don't know*?

ROSE. I don't know.

ARTHUR. Thank you. I did not claim this. I cannot know you. I
strive to, always, but alas I cannot. But my little dove, we are
human beings, bound together by something special. What is
that?

Answer me.

ROSE. I don't know.

ARTHUR. What ties you to me? A clue, my little Sherlock
Holmes – it is invisible, but very strong, even unbreakable,
like that fine empirical logic of yours.

ROSE. Blood?

ARTHUR. What is that you say? Speak up. Blood?

ROSE *nods*.

Actually? Or like a metaphor?

ROSE *shrugs*.

Do not shrug. A shrug is to gestures as sloths are to people.

ROSE. Like a metaphor. No, both.

ARTHUR. My clever little girl – you may yet become a poet as well as a mathematician. When you say blood, do you mean family?

ROSE *nods*.

So… I am your blood and you are mine?

ROSE. And Mummy's.

...

ARTHUR. Yes.

She is your blood.

But she is not mine.

ROSE. Why not?

ARTHUR. For we were not family – she was not my sister or my mother – but we *became* family… we were one… briefly… when you arrived, like a miracle, before she was… before she… But we are straying from the lesson, my little dove. It is late.

ROSE. I don't understand, what bound you to Mummy?

ARTHUR. Oh, a… a connection, a… a knot, yes, a knot, a very complicated knot – but it has an old-fashioned name, a simple word with too many meanings – do you know what it is?

ROSE. Why can't you just tell me?

ARTHUR. Because you have to feel it for yourself.

It binds you to me. I hope.

It binds you to your mother, I know.

...

ROSE. I know –

ARTHUR. Shhh, don't say it. Invisibility is its strength. You name it and it can vanish altogether, just when you least want it to, just when you need it the most. It is beyond our naming it.

So what did I claim?

ROSE. What, Daddy?

ARTHUR. What did I claim?

ROSE. I can't remember.

I really can't, I'm sorry.

ARTHUR. I claim not to know, but I do claim to feel.

Do I speak the gobbledygook?

ROSE *nods*.

Your mother used to say so. But listen to me once more and then you must clean yourself, take a paracetamol, drink some hot milk and go back to bed. Do you understand me?

ROSE. Yes, Daddy.

ARTHUR. Good good.

So I believe this –

When this invisible, unknottable, mysterious force exists between human beings, it can cause trouble and strife, but also happiness and wonder. So its simplistic name has become the most powerful word of all. So powerful it should not be said, but it's always there, on the tip of your tongue, because its effects are always felt. You hear me? *Felt*.

Second to this word in power is *knowledge*. But I may say this word, it does not reduce what knowledge is, for that is all it is, all we strive for – for words, for proof, for details. Knowledge is not human, it is outside of ourselves, it is the world around. So you revel in the *search* for it, don't you? For all that is not you. But many do not even search. They revel in ignorance, like hippopotamuses in their lakes of filth. But do you *feel* knowledge? I do not think so.

Knowledge is like an endless forest of trees you *use* to… to build a house, or a boat, or pulp to make a book. And you use that book to become a teacher, or a lawyer. Or a social worker. Or a judge.

Yes, a judge.

But do you use what is felt? I think not, my little dove. Feelings use you, I think. The invisible force uses you.

Pfft. Why am I telling you all this? Shut up, Arthur, boring, I'm tired, you're tipsy-tipsy, I want to go to sleep.

Because sometimes you… sometimes you… someone so much that if they hurt, you will hurt too. It is that simple.

So if my wife goes into the labour with my child and she suffers a terrible injury in the birth and she bleeds and bleeds and bleeds and then she dies, then I cannot *know* that pain, but I *felt* it. Like a cruel magic.

I *felt* it.

But I was wrong before. You are a woman almost – I see it in your eyes. Now you know exactly what happened to your mother. Now you know. Attend to yourself and rest, my little Rose, and tomorrow you will wake up a woman. This I know. *Inshallah*, as your mother would say.

…

ROSE. In what?

…

ARTHUR. Ah. Gobbledygook. Gibberish.

Sleep.

ARTHUR *turns and goes to his bed.*

He sits facing the window.

Scene Seven

Now.

The hospital.

Night.

Later.

Both in bed.

ARTHUR. Ooooo…

ROSE. I'm not asleep either, Arthur.

ARTHUR. Ooooo…

ROSE. I'm not getting out of bed. I'm fucking tired.

ARTHUR. Ooooo –

ROSE. I'd ask you what you want, but that's not going to prove very helpful, is it?

ARTHUR. Ooooo –

ROSE. Are you scared? Is that it?

   …

   I would be.

   I'm just over here, Dad. I'm not going anywhere. Look.

   She waves at ARTHUR.

   You see, here I am.

   Wave back. Go on, give it a go.

   ARTHUR *does – his left arm flops out of bed and he shakes it in her direction.*

   Nice one, Arthur – look at that.

   ARTHUR *tries to beckon her over.*

ARTHUR. Ooooo –

ROSE. I can't get into bed with you, I'm a grown woman, there wouldn't be room. And I don't want to sleep on that chair. I'm too old for that shit.

...

ARTHUR. Ooooo...

ROSE. I know what you want.

You want to know where I've been. You want to know why the fuck I'm here. You want to know how it's possible, after everything that happened.

Well, know this, Dad – this is impossible.

Happy?

Feel that.

Do you think I'm punishing you?

I don't mean to. I just think... you want me to be honest with you.

I'm being honest with you. I am.

Because you want to be honest with yourself now, don't you?

I'm only telling you things you already know.

Every word I say you've already heard. I promise.

How else could I say what I say? You're my dad.

I am you.

Aren't I?

Scene Eight

Thirteen years ago.

The bedsit.

Both in bed.

Midsummer.

Late, but the sun has just set.

ROSE *curled up, facing away from* ARTHUR, *listening to music on a radio next to her bed, the volume low. The music is chart pop,* circa *1998.*

ARTHUR *is reading the old hardback copy of* Romeo and Juliet.

He pours whiskey into the mug on his bedside table, then swigs from it.

He continues to read for a moment, then starts to drop off to sleep.

A new song starts on the radio. ROSE *turns it up.*

ARTHUR *jolts back awake.*

ARTHUR. What the devil?

Rose, what the devil is that cacophony? I tell you again and again, young lady, when the sun has set, time for more contemplative pursuits – read your books, write your diary, consider this and the next day's events –

ROSE. It's my radio, you gave it to me, I'm listening to it.

ARTHUR. It is too late for pop music –

ROSE. This isn't pop music.

ARTHUR. Yes it is, I am not a total fool –

ROSE. Could have fooled me.

ARTHUR. What's that?

ROSE. The name of the band, I just said what the name of that band was, alright?

ARTHUR. I did not ask you what the name of the band was – I do not care what the name of the band is –

ROSE. I said it isn't pop music, so I told you what band it is, alright?

ARTHUR. And they are not pop music?

ROSE. No.

ARTHUR. It is terrible.

ROSE. That's your terrible opinion.

ARTHUR. You are free to think that.

ROSE. And I'm free to ask you to keep your terrible opinions to yourself.

ARTHUR. Correct, this is a –

ROSE. Free country, England England England, Princess Di, Victoria sponge, blah blah blah, yeah, I know.

...

ARTHUR. You are a clever girl.

...

Please turn it down, you know the rules.

I ask you politely.

I am Mr Civility in this matter, young lady.

ROSE. You're drunk.

ARTHUR. What?

ROSE. I said you're drunk, Arthur.

ARTHUR. How dare you speak to me like that –

ROSE. You are –

ARTHUR. I am not –

ROSE. I don't even need to turn around, I can hear it in your voice –

ARTHUR. If you do not measure your language I will remove you from your bed in two shakes of the lamb's tail and teach you a lesson you will not forget in a very big hurry.

ROSE. I thought honesty was the policy.

ARTHUR. It is.

ROSE. And I must strive for knowledge.

ARTHUR. You must.

ROSE. And the truth will set you free.

ARTHUR. It will.

ROSE. Well, Arthur, I honestly know that the truth is that you're drunk, that you've finished most of that bottle of whiskey since I came home from school, and that I can smell it from here.

...

ARTHUR. Sherlock Holmes...

...

ROSE *sits up and pulls the bed curtain all the way around her bed.*

Why are you doing that?

Are you embarrassed of your father?

ROSE. Yes.

ARTHUR. Do I not make you proud? You make me swell with pride, like Moby Dick's whale.

ROSE. I don't know what you're talking about and I don't care about Moby's Dick.

ARTHUR. I should never have assembled that blasted curtain.

ROSE. It's the best birthday present I ever got.

ARTHUR. No...

ROSE. Yeah. It is.

ARTHUR. Better than the seaside?

ROSE. Definitely.

ARTHUR. Why?

ROSE. Why d'you think?

ARTHUR. Present your case, young lady.

ROSE. Don't make me say it, Dad –

ARTHUR. I am a grown man, I can take all your slings and arrows.

ROSE. Why can't you talk proper?

ARTHUR. I talk more *properly* than you, young lady, that is clear –

ROSE. I hate it, it's like you live in a Charles Dickens book or something – this is *1998*, Dad –

ARTHUR. Don't be idiotic –

ROSE. You want to know why I like it?

ARTHUR. What? I am lost.

ROSE. This curtain –

ROSE *shakes the curtain from inside it.*

This f… this brilliant, wicked curtain –

ARTHUR. 'Wicked'? It is a curtain –

ROSE. Because when I pull it around my bed I have my own room, Dad, my *own room*, but when I lie in my bed and see you lying in yours just over there I feel like I'm in *Oliver Twist* – I hate it, alright? I hate it – I can't ask any of my mates to come over –

ARTHUR. Of course you can –

ROSE. No I can't!

ARTHUR. Do not raise your voice with me – what are you ashamed of?

ROSE. What do you think? I live in a fucking one-room bedsit like a fucking tramp!

ARTHUR *swings out of bed, fully dressed, and storms towards* ROSE*'s bed, but does not pull back the curtain.*

ARTHUR. You never use that filthy language on me, you little
bloody bitch!

...

You hear me?

...

Come out here.

ROSE. No!

...

ARTHUR. I am sorry, please, Rose, my Rose, you are right, I
am drunk.

ROSE. No.

ARTHUR. No, no, I am. You are a clever girl, you are Sherlock
Holmes, I am drunk tonight – I had a long day –

ROSE. You don't have a job any more, Arthur.

ARTHUR. But I am… I am walking all day long, my Rose, all
day I am out on the streets of London looking for a job – I
promise – I went to every Waterstone's from here to Earls
Court –

ROSE. When are we going to get a proper flat?

ARTHUR. When I get a new job, when… when the council
selects us from their list –

ROSE. When?

ARTHUR. Please, my Rose, I am sorry, talk to my face like I
am a human being.

Please.

I am sorry we are still here. I thought you like it. I like it.

ROSE. How can you like this place?

ARTHUR. I like being with you. It is like a camping holiday. It
is home.

ROSE. I'm nearly sixteen, Dad, I need my own room.

ARTHUR. I am sorry.

ROSE. Whatever. Doesn't matter.

ARTHUR. I will make something up to you.

ROSE. What?

ARTHUR. I will recompense your discomfort.

ROSE. How?

ARTHUR. What would you like me to do? Think it like an early-bird birthday present.

ROSE. Anything?

ARTHUR. Ah… of course… No, not anything, I am not a magician, I am not a rich man –

ROSE. Something that don't cost money then?

ARTHUR. That would be… beneficial, yes.

ROSE. Do you promise?

ARTHUR. Well… if it cost no money and it is a present for my Rose, then yes! Anything! You may have anything!

As long as it costs no money – I only have ten quids left until giro day so I must scrimp and save –

ROSE *pulls back the curtain.*

She stands on her bed, holding a piece of paper.

She is wearing pyjama bottoms and a colourful T-shirt.

And her home-made hijab.

ROSE. There's this… this *disco* thing at school on Friday night –

ARTHUR. What…

ROSE. Like a dance or whatever, it's lame but everyone else is going so I want to, but I need your approval –

ARTHUR. What is…

ROSE. This is an approval form, I need you to sign it so I can go, because it's at this club that the school's hired out –

ARTHUR. You –

ROSE. Don't worry, there isn't any booze or anything, not that you should worry about that, because I don't drink, Arthur, because I'm a Muslim.

ARTHUR. What?

ROSE. I'm a Muslim, aren't I, can't you see?

ARTHUR. See?

ROSE. Yeah.

ARTHUR. I see a silly little girl standing on her bed with a badly made hijab on her head, waving a piece of paper in my face.

ROSE. So can I go?

ARTHUR. What?

ROSE. Go, can I go, to the school disco, on Friday?

ARTHUR. Yes, you may.

ARTHUR *turns away and walks back to his bed and sits facing the window.*

...

ROSE. Aren't you...

ARTHUR. What?

ROSE. Aren't you going to tell me to take it off?

ARTHUR. No.

...

ROSE. Why not?

ARTHUR. You are a Muslim, so you wear hijab.

ROSE. Yeah.

ARTHUR. Well done. Clever girl. Top marks.

ROSE. I am.

ARTHUR. So you say.

...

ROSE. I thought... I thought you'd be angry.

ARTHUR. I am too drunk to be angry. You timed your great revelation impeccably well. I am very gobsmacked. So I cannot speak.

...

ROSE. Fareeda says if I don't wear it all the time I'm not a good Muslim, so I even wear it when I go to school.

ARTHUR. Oh yes?

ROSE. Yeah.

ARTHUR. And do exciting things happen?

ROSE. What d'you mean?

ARTHUR. When you wear your hijab at school – do wonderful events occur?

ROSE. Nah.

ARTHUR. How disappointing. Will you wear it to the disco dance?

ROSE. Yeah.

ARTHUR. Have you been to a disco dance before?

ROSE. What? Um... no.

ARTHUR. Can you dance?

ROSE. What?

ARTHUR. Dance, can you dance?

ROSE. Yeah.

ARTHUR. Show me.

ROSE. What?

ARTHUR. Dance with me, come, it is an important lesson, even for a Muslim. Put on your radio, we will dance.

ROSE. No, Dad.

ARTHUR. I will not sign your form if you do not.

ROSE. You said you'd do anything that didn't cost money.

ARTHUR. I am renegotiating.

ROSE. That's not fair.

ARTHUR. Life is not.

> ARTHUR *switches her radio on.*
>
> *An inappropriate pop song plays out.*
>
> Excellent! This will do. Take my hand.
>
> Take my hand.
>
> *He takes her hand and puts his hand on her back.*
>
> *It is not a waltz, but nevertheless –*
>
> One two three, one two three –
>
> ARTHUR *launches into a catastrophic waltz step.*

ROSE. Dad!

ARTHUR. Keep going, you are a natural – yes! A natural Muslim disco-dancer!

> ROSE *breaks away and turns off the radio.*
>
> What is wrong?

ROSE. Just stop it, alright?

ARTHUR. What has happened to the world if a man cannot dance with his Muslim daughter?

ROSE. Shut up.

ARTHUR. You will do very well, the menfolk will be falling at your feet, God willing.

ROSE. Aren't you Muslim, Dad?

ARTHUR. Why you say that?

ROSE. You look like one.

ARTHUR. Do I?

ROSE. Yeah.

ARTHUR. How?

ROSE. Um...

ARTHUR. Is it my swarthy complexion?

ROSE. What?

ARTHUR. My bountiful, overflowing harem?

ROSE. What's that?

ARTHUR. I am sorry – please tell me how.

ROSE. You... you look like me.

ARTHUR. Ah.

But I do not wear the hijab.

ROSE. Men don't.

ARTHUR. You are correct. I was being – what is the word? Facetious. I am sorry. What then do you mean by I look like you?

ROSE. You're my dad.

ARTHUR. Yes... And? What?

ROSE. Not English.

ARTHUR. No, we do not *look* English, but you are.

ROSE. You're not, are you?

ARTHUR. I feel English.

ROSE. But you're not.

ARTHUR. You know that, don't you?

ROSE. Yeah.

ARTHUR. I feel otherwise.

ROSE. Where are you from, Dad?

ARTHUR. It is unimportant.

ROSE. It's important to me, I'm your daughter.

ARTHUR. Why?

ROSE. I need to know where I'm from.

ARTHUR. You were born in England, in the University College Hospital.

ROSE. Where were you born?

ARTHUR. I cannot remember, I was a baby.

ROSE. Why won't you tell me?

...

Why won't you tell me?

...

Why won't you –

ARTHUR. Because I swore to myself, I *swore* when you were
struggling your way into this world and your mother was
bleeding to death in front of me, that if you survived I would
give my heart to this country that had taken us in and forget
– never again even *speak* of the country that forced us out.

And I am a man of my word.

ROSE. What country?

ARTHUR. I know I am not English, but I feel it, is that not
enough? If you are English girl can I not be English man?

ROSE. No, Dad –

ARTHUR. Why? I speak like a gentleman, do I not?

ROSE. Because it's not true.

ARTHUR. Is it not? We look the same, don't we, my dove?

ROSE. Yeah.

ARTHUR. No. You look more like your mother.

ROSE. Do I?

ARTHUR. Yes.

ROSE. How?

ARTHUR. Biology. Puberty. You are now a woman in body and
I met her when she was a woman. In body. And in mind.

ROSE. Mum was a Muslim.

ARTHUR. Was she?

ROSE. What?

ARTHUR. I don't know.

ROSE. Course you do.

ARTHUR *lifts his pillow and takes out the folded hijab and places it at the bottom of the bed.*

ARTHUR. There she is, you ask her.

ROSE. What?

ARTHUR. Ask her.

ROSE. But –

ARTHUR. I talk to her every night, so no reason why you should not, she is your mother –

ROSE. What d'you mean?

ARTHUR. Maybe she is Muslim? Ask her.

ROSE. She's not there.

ARTHUR. Yes she is.

...

Yes she is, can't you see her? I can.

ROSE. You're scaring me, alright?

ARTHUR. Am I?

ROSE. Yeah.

ARTHUR. But I do speak to her, I do – I shut my eyes every night and I ask her questions, I ask her what am I to do with you, how should I be a good father to this English girl of ours, why did she leave us all alone like this, why why why why why why why, but I have never asked her is she Muslim. It is irrelevant to me. Psh. Maybe I should? Yes! Tonight! I will ask her tonight!

To the hijab –

Hello, my love, are you a Muslim?

ROSE. Stop it –

ARTHUR. Are you? Rose is – because she thinks you are too and she wants to be just like her mother, or what she thinks her mother might be, or what she wants her mother to be – an angel, a holy angel, one of the *Malā'ikah* –

ROSE. The what? –

ARTHUR. Perhaps Rose has had a visitation, my love, perhaps *Jibraaiyl* gifted her this wondrous revelation –

ROSE. Who?

ARTHUR. Perhaps *Mikaaiyl* has nourished her in her sleep –

ROSE. Stop it –

ARTHUR. Perhaps *Malak al-Maut* has taunted her with your death –

ROSE. Stop it!

ARTHUR. I thought you were Muslim, huh?

ROSE. I am!

ARTHUR. But the sun has just set and you were listening to your pop music.

ROSE. So?

ARTHUR. *Maghrib.*

ROSE. What?

ARTHUR. But now it is dark, but not yet midnight.

ROSE. Yeah.

ARTHUR. *Isha.*

ROSE. What?

ARTHUR. *Allahu Akbar.* [God is great.]

   ARTHUR *turns his head to the right.*

   Assalamu alaikum wa rahma-tullah. [Greetings be upon you.]

   He turns his head to the left.

   Assalamu alaikum wa rahma-tullah.

   ...

   Go to your disco.

   Go to your disco-dance with your hijab on. Why not? You must, for you are Muslim. You should.

   Hijab disco-dance...

   You have no idea what you talk of.

ROSE. Was that Arabic?

ARTHUR. It was gobbledygook –

ROSE. No it wasn't –

ARTHUR. Our Father who art in Heaven, hallowed be Thy name, Thy kingdom come, Thy will be done, in Earth as it is in Heaven –

ROSE. Stop it –

ARTHUR. Gobbledygook –

ROSE. No it's not –

ARTHUR. *abā-nā alladhī fī as-samāwāt-i,*

li-ya-ta-qaddas- ism-u-ka!

li-ya-'ti malakūt-u-ka! [The Lord's Prayer.]

It doesn't matter in what language – gobbledygook.

Jibraaiyl, Mikaaiyl, Malak al-Maut.

Gabriel, Michael, Azreal.

As you say – blah blah blah.

What do these things mean to you? What is this knowledge worth? How do you use it?

ROSE. I don't use it –

ARTHUR. Not yet, but I have taught it to you, so maybe it will have use, hmm?

Good. Maybe it will make you a *good Muslim* to know these things, believe these things. Whatever that means.

But you must believe what you wish. This is a free country. You have that choice. So choose and go forth my child – perhaps you may use this knowledge to choose a good Muslim man, perhaps you will find a good Jew, or a good Zoroastrian, or a good Christian, a good Copt, or just a good man. *God forbid* such a choice might bring you pain, might force you from your home. This is 1998, like you say, and who would care what you choose?

No one, I hope. No one.

Tell me, do you wear your hijab when you sleep?

Do you?

ROSE *shakes her head.*

Do you keep it under your pillow?

Answer me.

ROSE. Yes.

ARTHUR. So do I.

So do I.

ARTHUR *turns to the hijab, folds it up unsteadily and puts it under his pillow.*

He gets into his bed and turns off his light, turning away from ROSE.

She takes off her hijab and folds it, putting it under her pillow.

She gets into bed, pulling the curtain around her.

Darkness.

The sound of weeping.

Scene Nine

Now.

The hospital.

Night.

Later.

Darkness.

ROSE*'s curtain is closed.*

ARTHUR *moves in his sleep.*

ARTHUR. Aaaaaa…

…

Aaaaaa…

…

Aaaaaa!

Aaaaaa!

ROSE. Aaaaaa! Aaaaaaahmed!

ARTHUR *wakes with a start, looking around.*

…

ARTHUR. Aaaaa…

Aaaaa…

ROSE. She's not here.

ARTHUR *jumps in shock.*

ARTHUR. Ooooo –

ROSE. Fuck me, Dad, just when I'm about to drop off, there you go – aaaaaaaa….

It's like you'd rather I wasn't here.

It's like you'd prefer someone else to be here looking after you.

Funny that.

…

What's it like back home?

I know it's been a while since I've been there. I'm just wondering.

I imagine… not much has changed.

Have you kept my curtains up?

Are they still pulled around my bed?

Do you look at them and think, maybe she's there behind them? Maybe she came in late from Fareeda's house and I didn't hear the door.

Do you think, it's been so long now since she left I can't remember what she looks like?

Do you confuse me with someone else?

I would have come back if I could, Dad. I would.

But I've come now because you need me, don't you? You need me to help you get home.

Is that where you were going? Is it?

Ahmed?

Scene Ten

The bedsit.

Eleven years ago.

Early morning, just after dawn.

ARTHUR *is asleep, snoring.*

ROSE *pulls back the curtain and gets out of bed quietly.*

She pulls the curtain to.

She is wearing the same pyjama bottoms and T-shirt. Her hair is bedraggled.

She stumbles slightly.

She keeps her eye on ARTHUR, *careful not to make any noise, and walks to the door.*

She opens the door, exits and shuts the door.

ARTHUR *wakes at the noise of the latch.*

ARTHUR. Rose?

He looks towards her bed.

Rose? Are you here?

...

ARTHUR *gets out of bed and walks to* ROSE's *bed.*

He pulls back the curtain and looks inside.

ROSE *re-enters.*

ARTHUR *steps back*.

You are here.

ROSE. Correct.

ARTHUR. Where have you been?

ROSE. Why were you looking in my room?

ARTHUR. I was not looking in –

ROSE. You were –

ARTHUR. I was just seeing if you had come home –

ROSE. We agreed – that's my room – you knock on the door, remember?

ARTHUR. Yes –

ROSE. Like this –

ROSE *taps on the wall next to the curtain*.

ARTHUR. I know this –

ROSE. Or just call my name –

ARTHUR. Yes, or call your name –

ROSE. And if I don't answer then I'm not there, so you don't need to go snooping around my personal space –

ARTHUR. I was not snooping, I was worried –

ROSE. Why?

ARTHUR. I am your father –

ROSE. I am your daughter –

ARTHUR. So quick with your tongue – let me finish –

ROSE. I gotta be quick, haven't I? Otherwise I never get a fucking word in edgeways?

ARTHUR. You think you are all grown up, but I demand you do not use this filthy language in my house –

ROSE. Our *house*?

ARTHUR. Our *home*, my home – I am your father, you will respect my rules in this matter –

ROSE. Whatever, Dad, I'm going back to bed, it's like 6 a.m. or something –

ARTHUR. You hear my words, young lady?

ROSE. Yeah.

ARTHUR. You understand?

ROSE. No.

...

ARTHUR. What do you not understand?

ROSE. Give it a break, alright, Arthur?

ARTHUR. No, I do not give this a break, it is important to me – I know you do not respect me, but I have pride –

ROSE. Oh yeah?

ARTHUR. Yes indeed – I am proud to speak well and I thought I was proud to bring up a beautiful young woman who speaks like a true English lady –

ROSE. This is the year 2000, Dad, no one cares about true English ladies –

ARTHUR. I do –

ROSE. I know that, so why don't you go and find yourself one –

ARTHUR. Because I have one right here.

ROSE. No you don't.

ARTHUR. I can see underneath this bravado – I know what you are capable of –

ROSE. It's 6 a.m. It's *6 a.m.*

ARTHUR. I know what the time is.

ROSE. I. Don't. Want. To. Talk. About. This. Now.

ARTHUR. You are a troublesome teen, that is all. I will make us tea.

He walks to the back wall and pushes at it. A door, previously unseen, swings open onto a small messy kitchen. ARTHUR goes to the kettle.

ROSE. I don't want a cup of tea –

ARTHUR. But it is the morning – time for tea – nothing like a good brew to start the day – a thorough constitutional to reinvigorate the body politic, yes?

ROSE. I have no idea what you're talking about.

ARTHUR. Yes you do.

ROSE. I don't *want* to know what you're talking about.

ARTHUR. Ah, this I cannot change. But it is a shame. You used to.

ROSE. I'm going back to bed.

ARTHUR. Good luck.

ROSE. For what?

ARTHUR. Trying to get back to sleep.

ROSE. What does that mean?

ARTHUR. It means you may find it tricky.

ROSE. Why's that?

ARTHUR. It seems to me like a glorious day, I have the springer spaniel in my step, I feel excited and noisy, I feel a strong desire to converse with my daughter, for I have not seen her for three days.

For three days.

...

Where have you been?

...

Where have you been?

ROSE. It's none of your business.

ARTHUR. It is my business.

ROSE. Why?

ARTHUR. You are not yet of age, until then it is my business.

ROSE. I'm nearly eighteen –

ARTHUR. Nearly –

ROSE. I can do what I want –

ARTHUR. I do not wish you to leave your home, my Rose, but come your eighteenth birthday you can go where you wish, when you wish, but until then I am responsible for your well-being – jeepers-creepers how I wish it was not so – but it is the English *law*.

I know you have been to school.

ROSE. Did you phone college?

ARTHUR. Of course I did. I am glad you are at least keeping up with your studies.

ROSE. That's so embarrassing –

ARTHUR. I am an embarrassing individual, this I do not doubt. They tell me you are doing very well – I am pleased for you.

ROSE. What? You asked for a report?

ARTHUR. No no, I simply chatted with the lady in the office – what is her name?

ROSE. Jean.

ARTHUR. Yes, Jean, a charming lady – she told me you are much admired and are working very hard – I am proud of you, young lady, congratulations.

...

So at least I know wherever you have been you are still doing your homework.

Some habits die hard, yes?

ROSE. I was staying at Fareeda's, okay?

ARTHUR. Fareeda Banday?

ROSE. Yeah.

ARTHUR. She is your good friend, isn't she?

ROSE. Yeah, we go to the mosque together.

...

ARTHUR. Of course you do.

...

Why do you not bring her over for tea?

ROSE. I'm embarrassed, remember?

ARTHUR. Yes indeed.

I would be embarrassed if I were you.

I would.

We should live in a proper house. Oh, look at that, hooray hurrah, the kettle is boiled.

ARTHUR *goes to the kettle and makes two cups of tea.*

Do you enjoy mosque?

ROSE. What?

ARTHUR. Mosque. Do you enjoy it.

ROSE. None of your business, Dad.

...

ARTHUR. Would you like a crumpet or a muffin?

...

I said, would you like a crumpet or a muffin?

ROSE. No thanks.

ARTHUR. Are you sure?

ROSE. Yeah.

ARTHUR *puts some crumpets in the toaster.*

ARTHUR. I intend to start the day as I mean to go on. Sustained. Fuelled. Energised.

ROSE. Off to work?

ARTHUR. Yes indeedy. Here is your tea.

He hands ROSE *her tea. She takes the cup.*

...

Perhaps you will have a crumpet when it's in front of you. I think you may find it difficult to resist. I have Marmite on mine. I used to have honey, I know, but recently I tried Marmite again after many, many years and blow me down it was *delicious*. Did I ever tell you when I first tried Marmite?

Rose? Did I ever tell you when I first tried –

ROSE. No.

ARTHUR. It was soon after you had been born, I was in the hospital and had not eaten for maybe two days – I had not even thought of it – I don't know why – my head must have entered the fog for the first time – I do not know – anyway all of a sudden I had a cramp – horrible stomach cramps, I was so hungry. So I said to the nurse who was tending to you in your little glass box, 'Where can I eat in this blasted place?' She directed me to the hospital café, which I practically ran to, I was so ravenous.

The toaster pops up the crumpets.

Aha! Smell that. Scrumptious.

ARTHUR *sets about buttering the crumpets, then spreading on Marmite. When he's done, he brings them in and sets them down on the table and proceeds to eat them.*

As he does this –

So. I arrived and there were many other people there, including many husbands and wives, some with their newborn little ones, all of them eating hungrily. And I thought – Aha! To have a child must make you ravenously hungry! Yes, of course!

Stupid, I know. Foolish. I think perhaps I was deranged.

Possibly.

Mmm, this crumpet is delightful! Are you sure you do not want one?

ROSE *shakes her head.*

Your loss, my darling dove.

Where was I? Ah yes. So I lined up in the queue and there were so many choices, so many strange-looking foods I had never seen, so I turned to the man in front of me – a very thin, stringy man – no doubt starving for some food like me – I said, 'My friend, I am new in this fair country. My wife has just given birth to a beautiful girl, but then she died from a terrible bleeding injury – I am extremely hungry, what should I eat?'

He looked at me funny. Then he said, 'You have a Full English, mate.'

'A what?' I said.

'A Full English.'

And I was standing there staring at him, mystified, and he asked me, 'Are you alright, mate?' and I said 'Yes, thank you, I am all right,' and I ordered a Full English from the greasy-looking old lady behind the counter.

I waited with apprehension for some minutes, but then it arrived. Two slices of thick bacon, a Cumberland sausage, Heinz Baked Beans, two runny fried eggs the sunny-side up, grimy-looking oily mushrooms, a slice of that congealed pigs' blood and oatmeal sausage, and an enormous pile of toast.

And she gave it to me on a tray and its pungent aromas wafted up into my nose and… I was overcome… I began to cry – big sloppy tears into my Heinz Beans.

And then the lady said, 'Don't cry, dearie.'

I said to her, 'Many apologies, am I crying?'

And she said, 'Yes, you are, but don't be sorry – what's your name?'

And I did not know. I did not know my name.

So I said, 'My wife has just died. Her name is Warda.'

And she said, 'What does that mean?'

'Rose, it means Rose.'

'What a lovely name. Where does the name Warda come from?'

'It is Arabic for Rose. It is not *from* anywhere.'

'And what's your name then?'

And I knew then that I did not want my name any more, my dove. I did not want it. So I told her this, I said, 'I don't want my name any more, it is of no use to me now Warda is gone.'

And she said, 'Fair enough, duckie. So what shall we call you now, then?'

'I don't know,' I said.

'What names do you like?'

Then a man in the line behind me said he wanted to pay for his egg roll.

The lady behind the counter told him to f… off.

You know.

Then she said, 'Sorry about that.'

And I blurted out all of a sudden, 'I like very much the story of your King Arthur and his Round Table. I read this when I was a little boy and learning your beautiful language.'

And she laughed and said, 'Well, that sounds like a good English name to me, Arthur.'

And so she named me Arthur and I sat down and ate that Full English.

By golly gosh, it was delicious.

…

ROSE. What's that got to do with Marmite?

ARTHUR. What?

ROSE. What's that got to do with Marmite?

ARTHUR. Oh yes. On the toast – on the toast she had spread butter and Marmite. It was the last thing I ate as it smelt odious and by God it was *disgusting*.

…

ROSE. Mum's name is Rose.

ARTHUR. Yes.

ROSE. *Rose*. You always said I'm named after her, that she was called Rose too.

ARTHUR. She was.

ROSE. You just said her name was Warda.

ARTHUR. It is. It was.

ROSE. That's not the same as Rose.

ARTHUR. Yes it is.

ROSE. It's not the same word, Dad.

ARTHUR. No, but what's in a word?

ROSE. Everything, everything's in a word.

ARTHUR. I do not believe that.

ROSE. Then why are you called Arthur if that isn't your real name?

...

ARTHUR. You are a clever girl.

...

Do you enjoy mosque?

ROSE. It's none of your business.

ARTHUR. I hope you do, really I do –

ROSE. That's nice – did you enjoy mosque?

ARTHUR. What on earth do you mean?

ROSE. It's a simple question.

ARTHUR. Why is it you think I went to mosque?

ROSE. You're an Arab. I'm an Arab.

ARTHUR. Aha, of course, ergo mosque.

ROSE. I don't want to ask, Dad, I want you to tell me, I want you to *want* to tell me.

ARTHUR. I can't tell you, my Rose.

ROSE. I know, but why not?

ARTHUR. I will not tell you, I swore it.

ROSE. Where do think you're living, Arthur?

ARTHUR. What sort of question is this?

ROSE. A straight one –

ARTHUR. I sense it is not, I sense you are employing a rhetorical flourish –

ROSE. Shut your fucking mouth.

...

ARTHUR. What is that you say?

ROSE. Shut your fucking lying mouth.

ARTHUR. You will apologise.

ROSE. No.

ARTHUR. You are ruining our morning tea party – I am trying to build us a bridge –

ROSE. Go fuck yourself.

ARTHUR. I am not listening –

ROSE. Kiss my fucking arse.

ARTHUR. You say such ignoble statements – such degenerate language –

ROSE. This is how I speak –

ARTHUR. No it is not –

ROSE. Go fuck yourself, you fucking dune-nigger –

ARTHUR. What? What is this? Where do learn these despicable things?

ROSE. You fucking *kafir*-loving cunt –

ARTHUR. You are not too old to receive a sound beating –

ROSE. Come on then, you lying, duplicitous, two-faced, cuntlipped, raghead prick.

You sandy camel-eating, camel-toe fuckhead.

You failure.

ARTHUR *slaps her across the face*.

...

ROSE *punches him back. Hard.*

He falls back in shock.

...

What's in a word?

I want you to know something. I want you to feel something. Both, I want both. That's called *belief*. I want you to believe something.

I was going to tell you before. I was going to tell you yesterday.

I didn't stay at Fareeda's. Sorry, that was a lie.

ARTHUR. I know.

ROSE. Oh yeah?

ARTHUR. I phone Mrs Banday, her number is in the directory.

ROSE. I'm glad. I'm glad you know. Saves time. I woke up yesterday morning really early, as early as today – I'd been dreaming of Mum – not that I know what she looks like – there's no fucking photo, is there? I don't fucking know what my own mum looks like, Dad –

ARTHUR. We arrive here with very few possessions –

ROSE. Shut up – do you know what that's like, to not know your own mum's face? I've been dreaming about her you know – but that's impossible right? But not the *actual* her obviously, more this *sense* of her. In the dream it's like I'm on a treasure hunt or something – I'm running through this big city full of people – or I think it's a city, maybe it's a... a refugee camp – I can't really tell because there's a huge sun in front of me, like a desert sun, huge and hot, so fucking hot – and I'm running towards it, even though I can hardly stand the heat – and I can't stop running because I know that somewhere in that direction is my mum, somewhere near the sun. Fucking nuts, right? And something's chasing me, I don't know what, something's chasing me – and normally that's where I wake up – I wake up and I'm sweating from the heat of the sun and I'm screaming – and Danny has to calm me down –

ARTHUR. Who?

ROSE. Danny.

ARTHUR. Danny who?

ROSE. Danny Simpson. I've been staying at Danny Simpson's. Yeah. I can't sleep here any more, not since I've been having these dreams. I'm frightened of sleeping when I'm here – especially when you're screaming all night long –

ARTHUR. I do not scream –

ROSE. You do, Dad, it's fucking unbearable – and now I know what it is you're screaming – Waaaaaarda – Waaaaarda – I thought it was just fucking gibberish – gobbledygook, yeah? I feel so fucking stupid.

ARTHUR. Why do you not tell me I still scream?

ROSE. A nightmare noise, right? That's what you used to call it. That's true. That's a fact, Arthur. I've been screaming it too. Danny told me. It fucking freaked me out, you know – I was like, why am I screaming out that same weird fucking word? But now I know, don't I, Arthur?

Danny told me not to worry. I wake up and he holds me and then we *make love* and I'm not frightened any more – but I was scared yesterday morning and I'm still scared.

ARTHUR. Why?

ROSE. Cos the night before last I had the same dream again. I'm running, running, running towards that sun and the closer I get, the hotter it gets – crazy hot, like a fucking oven – normally that's where I wake up, but then for the first time the dream changed – I start to slow because I can't bear the heat any more and then I look down and I'm walking on hot sand and I'm barefoot and my feet are blistering –

ARTHUR. Stop this –

ROSE. And my body starts to shake –

ARTHUR. No –

ROSE. Really fucking shake –

ARTHUR. No no –

ROSE. And I look back up and the sun has turned into this…
this light bulb, yeah, this searing little light, like being right
up close to… to a *star*… but now it's like I'm in a tiny room,
like a cell –

ARTHUR. Stop this –

ROSE. And everywhere around me is wet and black, pitch
black –

ARTHUR. Please stop this –

ROSE. Yeah, black, apart from this little sun, this star, and then
the heat suddenly returns, it jolts through me, like electric
shocks –

ARTHUR. Aaaah –

ROSE. And I'm fucking shaking, Dad, all over – and then pop,
the light goes out –

ARTHUR. Aaaah –

ROSE *grabs* ARTHUR*'s face – he stops moving.*

ROSE. And then someone touches my face in the darkness… I
feel her caress my face and mop my brow… and I know it
must be Mum… or Allah… and her hand's so cool…

She lets go of him.

…

And then I woke up. Danny was holding me. I knew
something had happened. I knew it.

So I went down to Boots and got myself a test.

I'm pregnant, Dad.

…

ARTHUR. Danny Simpson?

ROSE. Danny Simpson.

…

I ran here, Dad. I ran here to tell you. Cos I'm fucking
terrified, right?

He goes to try and embrace her.

She moves away.

Nah, nah, no you don't.

I got to the end of the street – yesterday morning, about eleven o'clock – and saw you come out of the front door. You looked funny, off-key. I thought you were drunk. You walked a few paces into the street, didn't you?

Then you stopped and looked around. You gazed up at the sky and shielded your eyes from the sun, like you hadn't seen it for days. Some big fat bald guy bumped into you and you stumbled back.

Then you looked around some more. Squinting. I couldn't figure out what you were looking for.

Then you went back inside.

And then I knew, Dad. I just knew. You never really leave, do you? Do you? You send me off to school and then you just…

I waited around for an hour in the café.

You came out again at around one-ish, got as far as the Post Office – then turned back and went back inside.

At three, you got as far as the off-licence and bought a bottle of Jameson's.

You're still trying, though, still *searching,* aren't you, Arthur? Because you know you should, but something keeps dragging you back.

At four I went back to Danny's.

You know what? You don't need to tell me where you're from. Because you live there all the time. Don't you? You're there right now.

…

So don't tell me. I don't need to know.

I've had a hole inside of me my whole life, but now something is filling it up.

ARTHUR. A little Englishman.

   ...

ROSE. Yeah, a little Englishman.

Scene Eleven

The hospital.

Later.

The half-light before dawn.

ARTHUR *in bed, awake, staring at the other bed, the curtain of which is again pulled fully round.*

We hear ROSE *jumping up and down on the bed. Occasionally her hijab covered head is seen popping over the top of the curtain.*

ROSE. Whoo!

Do you remember when I used to do this when I was little? When I got up in the morning? Fuck me, I used to love going to school, couldn't wait to get out of that fucking shoebox.

She stops.

Is that the sun rising?

I can feel it getting warmer.

You haven't screamed again tonight, Arthur, well done. Are you feeling more peaceful? I hope so. I am.

Here's a *Countdown* conundrum for you – if I can't go to school today – I mean, I'm too old right? – so if I can't go to school and I'm getting excited and jumping up and down on the bed... where can I possibly want to go?

Danny Simpson's?

Nah, can't go there.

Fareeda Banday's?

Nope. Fuck, she annoyed me – so fucking precious. She was right though. I'm not a very good Muslim, am I, Dad?

My heart's in the right place though.

Same place as your heart, I think. What d'you reckon?

I'm getting off-track. Back to the puzzle.

Where can I possibly go?

Maybe I'll go and see my little baby.

ARTHUR. Ooooo…

ROSE. Exactly. Noooo. I can't do that. I don't know where she is.

I know it's a she though. Definitely.

…

Do you feel like going away somewhere?

How about a trip to the seaside, would you like that?

ARTHUR. Ooooo…

ROSE. Don't worry, I'm just teasing, Dad. I know where you want to go.

…

ROSE *pulls back the curtains.*

She is standing on the bed.

She wears her hijab.

And her bloodstained nightie.

ARTHUR. Ooooo!

She gingerly jumps down and walks to ARTHUR*'s bed.*

ROSE. Calm down, it's alright.

ARTHUR. Ooooo!

ROSE. What? I don't have anything else to wear.

She picks up the folded trousers from the chair.

She fishes around in one pocket and pulls out a thick wad of cash – several hundred pounds at least.

Hello hello…

Jackpot.

What's all this for?

She fishes in the other pocket and pulls out a passport – not a British one.

Going on holiday, Dad?

…

You were off to the airport, weren't you?

He nods.

I know.

You've been reading the papers, haven't you?

He nods.

Watching the TV?

He nods.

I bet you couldn't believe it – after all these years.

You don't need to tell me. I know what you know, don't I?

He nods.

Yeah.

Because I'm you. So I know they wouldn't let you and Mum be together. A Christian and a Muslim? That's not possible, is it? You didn't care though. You only cared for each other.

So your father disowns you, your brother won't speak to you… and Mum's family… And when you got her pregnant… They told their friends in the police… they did those things to you… But they couldn't beat it out of you, could they? That word on the tip of your tongue. It's still there, isn't it?

No wonder you flew away to this green and pleasant land.

But you're right, you know. I couldn't have understood. But you should have told me. You know that, don't you?

He nods.

Because then I would have known it and then maybe I would have felt it and then, somewhere in between the two, I would have believed it. And that's what's important, isn't it?

He nods.

She strokes his head.

Oh, Dad, you worked yourself into a right old fucking frenzy, didn't you? You couldn't believe your eyes – everything you ran away from crumbling in front of you – but you weren't there, you were in that horrible fucking room, glued to the TV… and that wouldn't do, would it, Dad?

He shakes his head.

You packed your bag and you made it all the way down the high street for the first time in ten fucking years and then…

She puts her finger to his head.

Pop.

Listen.

…

Can you hear the screaming?

He shakes his head.

I can.

It's a long way away.

She shows him the passport.

This far away.

Come on, Dad, take my hand.

Arthur, stop fucking about, take my hand.

He takes her hand.

Up you get.

She pulls him and he – very lightly – steps out of bed, fully dressed.

The heart monitor flatlines silently.

Well done. Look at you, always so smart.

ARTHUR. Ooooo –

She puts her fingers on his lips.

ROSE. Shhh. You've done plenty of that. Keep your trap shut.

Do you hear it now?

…

ARTHUR *nods.*

That's right. They're just like you. They've been screaming their whole life, but it's only now you've woken up.

She walks to the back wall and pushes against it. The hidden door swings open once again, but this time there is no kitchen, just empty space.

She looks out and back at ARTHUR.

That's where you're from. That's where you're going –

Warda.

ARTHUR *walks to the door, looks back at* ROSE.

She climbs onto her bed and pulls the curtains around her.

ARTHUR *looks out*

ARTHUR. Warda.

He exits.

Scene Twelve

The bedsit.

As before.

Ten years ago.

Night.

Dark.

The front door opens and ARTHUR *walks in.*

He is clutching a hijab.

He walks in and stands in the middle of the room, staring into space.

He takes off his jacket – it drops to the floor.

His shirt is covered in blood.

So are his hands.

He looks around.

He sits on his bed.

He sees the closed curtain.

He walks to ROSE*'s bed and pulls back the curtain.*

No one there.

He sits on ROSE*'s bed, clutching her hijab.*

He lays the hijab on the bed.

He carefully, tenderly, folds it up.

He lifts her pillow and places it underneath.

He pulls the curtains around him.

A distant sound of a baby screaming and crying.

The End.

Acknowledgements

Thanks to the following for their assistance, advice, encouragement and wisdom... My parents and brothers, Dina Shoukry, Dr Andy and Dr Ruth Lyon, Ziad Khuzai and Sammer Khatlan, Nirjay Mahindru and everyone at Interact Reading Service (www.interactreading.org), John Heffernan, Ben Woolf, Myanna Buring, Lily Williams, Alex Waldmann, Amelia Sears, Abbey Wright and Jess, Art and Keira Malik for asking me.

Hywel John

A Nick Hern Book

Rose first published in Great Britain as a paperback original in 2011 by
Nick Hern Books, 14 Larden Road, London W3 7ST, in association with
Dirty Boots, MLJ, SEArED and Pleasance Theatre

Rose copyright © 2011 Hywel John

Hywel John has asserted his right to be identified as the author of this work

Cover image: photography by Corin Hardy / design by Ben King
Cover design: Ned Hoste, 2H

Typeset by Nick Hern Books, London
Printed in the UK by CLE Print Ltd, St Ives, Cambs, PE27 3LE

A CIP catalogue record for this book is available from the British Library

ISBN   978 1 84842 224 7